The
ROARING
RAINBOW

poems for children

by
DENNIS
CARTER

To Catrin with best wishes from Dennis Carter 19.6.13

Illustrated by
Aunt Alga

catchfire publications

September 2010

Pentre Farm, Woodhill, Oswestry,
Shropshire. SY10 9AS
phone: 01691 656320
email:
dennisbcarter@hotmail.com

ISBN 978-0-9533499-8-2

Dennis Carter lives in Shropshire with his wife. Their children have all left home now but their cats are still there. Dennis visits many primary schools in Wales and England doing poetry and story workshops with children of all ages. He enjoys performing his poems and sometimes even breaks into song.

Aunt Alga lives in North London. She has two brown cats and one pink baby. She likes drawing, painting and digging holes.

Other poetry collections
by Dennis Carter

SLEEPLESSNESS JUNGLE (1998)

ON THE RAZZLE DAZZLE (2001)

SHINY METAL WORDS (2005)

DANCE WITH THE MOON (2007)

Novels for children
by Dennis Carter

MISSPELLBOOBILAND (1999)

BRINGING HOME THE DEAD (2003)

THE SLEEPING FORCE (2009)

Thanks to all the headteachers who have invited me into their schools to teach poetry to the children in recent years; to the BBC for their permission to publish my poems which appeared in the CBeebies programmes 'Poetry Pie', broadcast in 2009: Dandelion Clock, Happy Picture, My Knife, Fork and Spoon, and Our Cat; to Aunt Alga for her wacky illustrations and last but not least to the children in the schools who have listened and responded to these poems.

A BABY'S COMING
(for Ollie Bennett)

"A baby's coming,"
said the little boy
to the blue sky and
the sparrows flew up
in a whirring cloud.

"A baby's coming,"
said the little boy
to the orchard trees
and their branches shone
with bright red apples.

"A baby's coming,"
said the little boy
to the strutting hens
and they clucked and whined
with joy in the field.

"A baby's coming,"
said the little boy
to his daddy's friends
and they sipped their tea
with pleasure in the sun.

THE TEAPOT

I know an old and
pleasant lady
who cuddles her
teapot like a baby.

She rocks it left
and rolls it right
and soon to every
one's delight

she fills each cup
with tea that steams
and fills each head
with happy dreams.

But when she's washed
and dried that pot
does she I wonder
pop it in its cot?

NAME CALLING

You are nice, nice as rice
pudding on the table
after Sunday roast.

You're just right, right and bright
as a bobbing boat
sailing near the coast.

You are sweet, sweet and neat
as honey, jam or treacle
on my breakfast toast.

You are great, great as a mate
let us play together -
I like you the most.

LIGHTNING

Lightning
paints the trees
with sudden silver

leaving only dark
and a distant grumble.

GRANDPA THE DRUMMER

I've seen drum kits at a concert,
such fancy drums to play
but anything can be a drum
when Grandpa comes to stay.

Pop drummers love their cymbals,
their snare drums and their sticks
but anything can be a drum
when Grandpa's at his tricks.

He taps his toes on floor tiles
and bangs his heels on stone
and anything can be a drum
when Grandpa's not alone.

He drums with thumbs at breakfast –
he drums when eating food
for anything can be a drum
when Grandpa's in the mood.

He rattles on the windows
and patters arms of chairs
for anything can be a drum
when Grandpa comes downstairs.

He drums with perfect timing,
he drums both quiet and loud
and anything can be a drum
for Grandpa, old and proud.

WIND
Wind makes
everything sing.
Tall trees sing
of wishes made,
pink and blue
and wave their
magic wands so
they come true.
Wind is so
ring-a-ding-ding!

WINTER MOSQUITO

It must have come here
in a summer invasion,
perhaps out of Africa
or maybe it's Asian.

With bendy long legs
and small silky tail on
it looks like something
from the film called Alien.

Buzzing round my head
when I'm watching telly,
it injects my ankle, my
cheek and my belly.

You're wasting your time
if you try to swat it.
Whenever you grab it
you've never really got it.

Granny says it needs
a heavy frost on it.
Dad says it really needs
a rock tossed on it.

When Mum sprayed the room
with a kind of chemical
its dying antics
were kind of comical.

FROG

Frog is a blob
of green and brown,
a squat in the wet
but oops, when I touch

frog is a hop
with goggled frown
a leap away, yet
I didn't touch much.

OLD MAN

Old man walks
down memory lane
not so quickly
now he's lame.

MY KNIFE, FORK
AND MY SPOON

One day my knife
Sliced through my chip.
Silver was the knife
And golden the chip.

Next day I used
My knife like a digger
And squashed my peas
To make them bigger.

One day I held my
Fork near and high.
It looked like a cage
Was around the sky.

Next day I put my
Fork on my plate.
It looked like the bars
On our garden gate.

One day I gazed at
The back of my spoon
And it showed my face
Like a fat balloon.

Next day I saw the
Other side instead.
What a surprise when
I stood on my head!

PREGNANT WOMAN
Calmly she walks
and carries her pack
down on her front
not up on her back.

FLY
Fly sits in the sun
rubbing his hands with glee,
wondering who next to annoy.
Is it you or is it me?

SUMMER
Heat waved once
and flew away.
Rain cried twice
then came to stay.

BLACK ARROWS
AT HEATHROW

At the airport terminal
whichever way you go
watch out for the deadly
black arrows, black
arrows on yellow boards,
pointing down,
pointing up,
pointing left ,
pointing right

but when you're desperate
the black arrow to the toilet
is nowhere to be seen,
pointing down,
pointing up,
pointing left ,
pointing right

If you discover that
flying dart, it's pointing up.
Perhaps you must find the
invisible rope ladder,
faintly silver, leading

right into the ceiling
and very slowly
climb up then tap
the panel at the top.

It smoothly opens
and shows the toilet
gleaming white
among cobwebs
and bat droppings.

WAITING

Crouched like
a grasshopper
an old man in
a yellow cap
taps and twirls
a wooden stick
over the tiles
as if trying to
discover a
source of
water.

MY MATE JOHNNY

Whenever I think of Johnny
I see fair hair like the roof
of a cottage, large teeth like
standing stones, sea blue
eyes and whispered jokes –
Johnny's jokes, dry
and hilarious.

Whenever I think of Johnny
I recall Popeye impersonations.
He'd do rough-voiced Popeye
"I's a comin' Olive" and I'd do
Bluto's double bass, "I'll fix
that little runt Popeye".
He'd do Sweapea and Wimpy
and I'd do Olive Oil screaming,
"Popeye, Popeye, save me,
save me!"

Whenever I think of Johnny
I remember cold nights on
the terraces of Rovers F.C.
when we should have been
at night school but also
warm nights under the stars
in wild places after
climbing mountains and
fording streams.

BUD

In a pale covering
of faceted armour
Bud your body waits,
your light glimpsing
through Tree's dark.
Soon your green
glance unwrinkles
a tight muscle.
Next a wet finger
prods gingerly
to find which way
the wind and a soft
hand opens to give
us each a present:
dangling spring.

CONKER

No polish, however rare
could neither burnish nor restore
the quickly fading sheen
fresh out of the split husk
of the spiky conker shell.

LEAVES

One leaf fell
like a bird
fluttering.

Two leaves fell
like old men
muttering.

Three leaves fell
like squirrels
scuttling.

Four leaves fell
like laughter
chuckling.

Five leaves fell
like yellow
ducklings.

SUMMER'S
GONE BLUES

Summer's gone
and Autumn's coming.
Winter soon
and weather slumming.

Rags of cloud
all grim and dirty
very soon
are wet and squirty.

Messy winds will
chuck their litter,
flying things
to patter and pitter.

Birds will fluff
and seek for shelter
when the roads
turn helter-skelter.

Temperatures
have dipped to zero.
Go outside and
be a hero.

OUR CAT

Most days I love
our warm and wafty,
our smooth and softy
cat very much.
She lets me give her a cuddle.
She comes to me for a snuggle.

Some days I don't like
our sly and sneaky,
our mean and cheeky
cat very much.
She's just a little pest today.
She licked my dinner yesterday.

Most days I love
our sleek and slinky,
our dainty dinky
cat very much.
She's cute even when she's creeping.
She purrs even when she's sleeping.

MISS THORNTON

If I imagine very hard I see
my teacher from years ago,
Miss Thornton, red haired
Miss Thornton smiling and
if I keep imagining she
becomes a beautiful red
geranium in a terracotta pot.

Miss Thornton, loveliest
of teachers, comforted me
when I was late for school
one day, the only day
I was ever late and my
mummy brought me crying
into the classroom to red
haired Miss Thornton.
"It's alright, Dennis," she said,
"wipe your tears away and
sit in your place for reading."

I look at Miss Thornton,
moist eyes soon drying.
She smiles at me in sympathy
and her geranium face
bursts into fragrant flowers.

SAND

Wet grains turning
dry in the constant wind
lift into low tides of sand
as sea retreats.

Solid ground loses
its surface, its small
shards, airborne at no
more than ankle's height,
rush away to the land
as if escaping, fixing
themselves like little
silver ants in swarms onto
obstacles: stubborn rocks
are softened and glittered;
castaway branches
have their twigs thickened
into pointing fingers;
isolated rushes
build into islands.

The islands of sand
are joined to make dunes
soon crowned with sea
holly's purple flowers.

TORTOISE AND HARE

Walking away
from the aeroplanes
the young man
strides out, pulling
his heavy luggage
as if it is nothing

but creeping along
the moving footpath
the very old man
hobbling on a stick
soon overtakes him.

STORM

Wild winds
call, call.
Rain, hail
fall, fall.
Fresh gales
squall, squall.
Tossed trees
tall, tall,
crash down
all, all.

HAPPY PICTURE

I painted a picture
and Happy is its name.
Miss Richards loves it
and put it in a frame.

In the sky the sun is bouncing
like a ball with a cheeky grin
and underneath is a tall green tree
with juicy fruits and birdies in.

I painted a picture
and Happy is its name.
Miss Richards loves it
and put it in a frame.

Next to the tree is my big house,
roof and windows and red front door.
In the garden are yellow flowers
and jumping rabbits on the floor.

I painted a picture
and Happy is its name.
Miss Richards loves it
and put it in a frame.

If you look closely you'll see me
swinging high from the tall green tree.
Mummy is walking down the path
and look there's Daddy pushing me.

FOSSIL

This rock is really a grave
of a long lost water creature.
His legs are oars,
his ribs a cage
and he once lived
in a bygone age.

His skeleton is saved,
perfect in every feature.
His head's a spear,
his ribs a cage
and he once lived
in a bygone age.

THE WITCH IN MY DREAM

The wicked witch in my dream
turns with her spells all I've seen
into nightmares, into night scares
into dreadful scenes.

"Abracadabra!" she cursed
and five friends became four.
"Hocus pocus!" she shrieked
and Christmas was no more.

"Shazam!" then she shouted
and birthday candles dimmed.
"Mumbo jumbo!" she moaned
all joy and smiles grimmed.

"Gobbledegook!" she gabbled
and bad thoughts filled our minds.
"Jiggery-pokery!" she jabbered
as she pulled down the blinds.

That wicked witch in my dream
turns with her spells all I've seen
into nightmares, into night scares,
into dreadful scenes.

DANDELION CLOCK

A puff of fluff
like a feather flies
from the stem
so soft, so soft.

A puff of fluff
like a parachute falls
to the grass
so light, so light.

A puff of fluff
like a snowflake melts
in the earth
so quiet, so quiet.

A puff of fluff
like magic makes
a new flower
so bright, so bright.

BUTTERFLY

Who taught
the butterfly to fly?

Was he some
kind of funny guy?

Look at that
brown one, no idea

of straight lines
and no second gear,

only that silly
quivering

and that crazy
dithering.

Whoever taught it
flight like that

must be wearing
a funny hat!

SCHOOL RUN

If you're sat inside a car
you are never going far.
If you're walking in the street
you must watch for both your feet.
If you're playing in the park
you'll be there until it's dark.

School run, School run
what a scrum - it's no fun
getting gobbled up
by the School Run!

Here it comes that armoured tank
tail to bumper clank, clank, clank.
Here it comes that long blue snake
showing teeth and spitting lakes.
Here it comes that flabby whale
blowing bubbles, swatting tail.

School run, School run
what a scrum - it's no fun
getting gobbled up
by the School Run!

There it goes that crazy crowd
chanting insults very loud.
There it goes that shower of rain
spreading down the town again.
There it goes to many homes
leaving sighs and moans and groans.

School run, School run
what a scrum - it's no fun
getting gobbled up
by the School Run!

AUTUMN 1

The leaf that scuttles
across the street
near our house
is a mouse.

The leaf that flutters
out of the tree
and back again
is a wren.

WINTER
All the plates
and all the cups,
all the saucers
and all the jugs,
all the plaques
and all the tiles
of summer are
broken crockery.

ED'S HEAD
When he's in bed
in Ed's head
are one bird,
two words,
three trees,
four seas,
five dogs,
six logs,
seven goats
eight ghosts,
nine streams,
ten dreams
in Ed's head
when he's in bed.

THREE STRANGE MEN

Man One is so freaky
with a blue face and
a star on his cheeky,
a red beard and hat of
speckles, licking
a square ice cream.

Man Two's a soldier
with an insect snout
and a single spinning
eye like Cyclops, who
wears a large black hat
with a blue feather
flying from it down
to his blood red cape.

Man Three's a sad hippy
whose lippies are black
tulip buds and eyes
as dark as outer space
whose long fair hair
has green stripes.
Tramlines run across
his forehead but all
the trams are empty.

ANT

Little black and shiny ant
always hurrying.
What busy jobs and missions
send you scurrying

up your stick or stem of flower
and down again
sometimes with tiny parcels
in the sparkling rain?

I saw you meet another ant
one day to chat
with long feelers softly touching
this way and that.

Soon after you said, "Goodbye"
with final touches
and ran away with your burden
to the bushes.

MAN ON A BIKE

A man I saw on a bike
and what did he look like?
He wore a beard
so grey and long.
He did not look
so very strong.

That old man riding away
what on earth did he say?
He sat up high
as on a horse.
He shouted loud
till he went hoarse.

That shouting bicycle man
where did he go to then?
He went quiet
like a mouse.
He rode into
his little house.

WENDY'S POEM

Little Wendy
wrote a poem.
She wrote it
from her heart.

After she finished
the last line
the page waved
and started
to fly, so good
was that poem.

Wendy's teacher
put it in a box
to stop it flying
away and pressed
firm the lid.

In the night
the box floated
gently to the stars.

THE OLD FORGE

An age defamed.
 The forge declined:
dreams and death in its dark stones;
fading shadows in its fire-realm;
haunted its rust-hoard.
 Hands of light
touch old treasures, trace the glory
of hung tools and horse-shoes
briefly until they bring the dark.

The wealth is all wasted; wheeze no
more breaths through leather bellows;
silenced is the anvil and vanquished
the hammering hands, now held by earth.
No coals glow, for cold rules here.
That mighty furnace, famous for ages,
that roared and melted the rigid iron,
was choked one day with cheerless waste.
Ripped packages, polythene tumours,
cans cast away were crammed inside
and pulled into place by a bent pole.

The dominion of the smith is destroyed.
Times are tired. The titans have gone.

GREEN

In all the haze of spring
From dancing yellow
to wedding white,
Green descends.
You cannot keep
down the surging
Green as if water
needs colour and
finds it in green.

Green, green, the strumming theme,
making lovely what was mean.

Witchcrafty, creeps Green,
casting spells over
the grey of winter.
Touch the ground:
ground is Green.
Flick the tree:
tree is Green.
Stroke the hedge:
hedge is Green.

Green, green, the strumming theme,
making lovely what was mean.

OLD LADY,
SWIMMING

Study the water,
feel it, not too bad,
down the steps,
ease in, ease in.
Aaah! Oooh!

Off into a polite
breast stroke with
barely a splash.
Not a hair on her
head yet wet,
nor even a spot
on her calm face.

Pause at the shallow
end for a little rest
and off again as
a small smile opens
like a bright water lily.
Weightless, she
feels she's flying,
delighting in her
precise breaststroke.

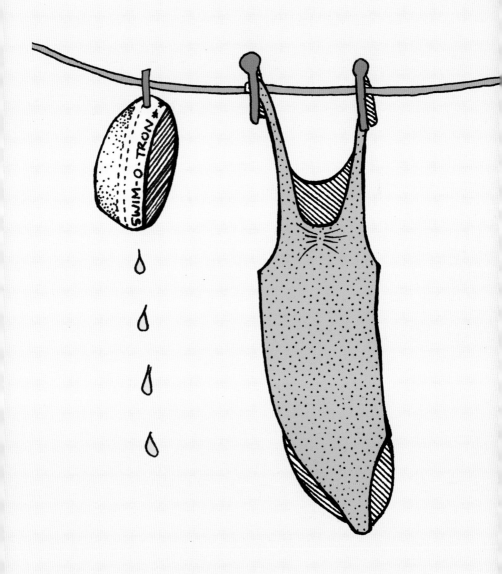

CHICKS

In their smooth shells
silently the eggs rest
under the hen's feathers
in a soft nest.

Warm and broody
the mother hen sits tight
caring for her precious
ones day and night.

Inside the smooth eggs
yellows grow red spots.
Spots turn to lumps,
lumps into skinny tots.

With their tiny hammers
the new chicks poke
out into the new world –
so lovely to stroke.

SOFT

Soft as the tuft
of feathers on
the breast of a swift

or a sift of sand
or a drink of milk

or a shift in the land
or a dress made of silk.

CHEWING

If chewing were thinking
all cows would be philosophers.
If thinking were chewing
all philosophers would be fat.

BIRDS

Mild-eyed and mottled
Dunnock comes to call.
Red-eyed and throttled
is Pheasant's harshest call.

BOUNCY CASTLE

Bouncy castle,
castle's bouncy
makes me feel all
flouncy, pouncy.

When I run on it
I'm having fun on it.

When I jump on it
I'm a flying lump on it.

When I drop on it
I flippity flop on it.

When I roll on it
I'm toad in the hole on it.

Bouncy castle,
castle's bouncy
makes me feel all
flouncy, pouncy.

STUCK IN
A MARSH

Caramel fudge –
my legs slither right in
and reeds soon tickle my chin.

Sticky toffee sludge –
boots fill up to the brim
with water brown and grim.

Milk chocolate mudge –
splats and sploshes my face
and now I look a disgrace.

Feet cannot budge –
suction-locked in the mud.
I'd pull 'em out if I could.

THE PAST

How fast the past is made.
The batsman's century
and the striker's hat trick
drop into the record books
as we think of the next game.

JEREMIAH THE CAT

Jeremiah is a timid little cat.
When he hears a shout
he shoots straight out;

when he sees a stranger
he knows it's danger;

when the light goes on
in a flurry see him run;

when he hears loud bumps
to the moon he jumps.

But is Jeremiah a timid little cat?
When he sees birds' flutters
he growls and mutters;

when he hears grass rustle
he 'll hustle and bustle;

when he comes in the house
he's playing with a mouse;

and do not say a word
now he's eating up a bird!

VEGETABUBBLES
(for Ollie Robarts)

Forget your pains and
forget your troubles.
Simply tuck into
your vegetabubbles.

Don't pull a bad face
don't be mean
simply slurp down
the shiny baked bean.

And that green bush
that sits so jolly
on your plate is
steamy broccoli.

Now is the time for
a crunchy carrot
looking like the orange
beak of a parrot.

But best of all
is mashed potato
fluffed and buttery
on your plato.

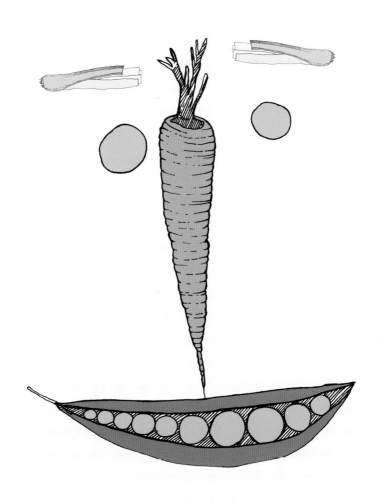

Not forgetting peas
and parsnips,
cabbages, leeks and
crispy large chips.

Forget your pains and
forget your troubles.
Simply tuck into
your vegetabubbles.

BLACKBIRD

Blackbird
fine bird
around eyes
golden rings
ding and dong
golden song
golden sings
never sighs
fine bird
Blackbird.

WHITE BIRD

White bird, white bird
of the muddy marshes
who washed you dazzling clean?

Which powder was used
and what's it like
inside a washing machine?

HAIKU

It drank the sunset,
nibbled the moon and the mist -
the cock bullfinch.

Crescent moon in clay
remembers trot or canter -
hoofprint of a horse.

Little mice in boats
could sail high seas of the school -
morning of the flood.

HAWK DREAM

A hawk was trapped in my bedroom; yellow
was his brow, grey and blue his sleek feathers.
What should I do about the hawk with his
long legs and claws like knives, his clear patterns
and those ferocious eyes? Carefully I crept to
where he perched, on the bedpost next to
my striped pyjamas, carefully I crept
and quietly, quietly until I could almost
touch him. The hawk shuffled and stared at me,
interested not scared at all so I took
him into my hands. Oh, did he bite me!
His hooked beak dug into my hand, but then
the pain left me as I lifted the hawk
to the window, where flocks of little birds
glared hard at him with their bold, shining eyes.
They pecked at him out of fear and anger,
then the hawk no longer wanted to leave
my hands or the room or my world that is
so different from his. He turned away from
freedom outside, fluttering in panic
into my arms all soft and warm. I looked
at him. But now he was no bird, only
a boy, dark-eyed and scared in the night time.

WHATEVER HAS HAPPENED TO GWEN?

Whatever has happened to Gwen
who always walked alone,
pushing her pram full of shopping
like one of the Unknown?

Whatever has happened to Gwen,
who wore a long black coat
in every weather and season
buttoned up to her throat?

Whatever has happened to Gwen
whose house was down the street,
with trees, weeds and brambles
reaching for passing feet?

Whatever has happened to Gwen
who never spoke a word
nor ever looked at passersby
so deep in her own world?

Whatever has happened to Gwen
who is no longer there,
walking the streets of the old town,
no one seeming to care?

Whatever has happened to Gwen
who died one summer's day?
People were asking this question
but Gwen had gone away.

AUTUMN 2

Can you catch
a beech tree's falling coin
before it hits the ground?
If you can, be healthy.

*Catch it, catch it,
catch it if you can.*

Can you catch
a beech tree's falling coin
and hold it in your hand?
If you can, be wealthy.

*Catch it, catch it,
catch it if you can.*

THE GREAT BUS

The great bus roars.
The bus leaves the kerb
and is roaring like
a bad tempered bear.

The great bus roars.
The bus leaves passengers
and is roaring as
if it doesn't care.

The great bus roars.
The bus frightens grown ups
like the young mother
who pushes her pram.

The great bus roars.
The bus scares children
who dodge and dive
to avoid a slam-bam.

The great bus roars.
The bus jumps and hisses,
preparing to roar for
mile after mile.

The great bus roars.
The bus stops and waits
for the blind old lady
wearing a smile.

SIX PEBBLES

'Ploosh!' said the first pebble
to the sea's wobbly face.
'Oops!' said the second pebble
in a wave's cool embrace.

'Clip-clop!' said the third pebble-
did a horse ride the sea?
'Stomach!' said the fourth pebble
was this one expecting tea?

'Gulp!' said the fifth pebble
as the large wave swallowed it.
'Oo-ooh!' said the sixth pebble-
for it felt the cold a bit.

LITTLE POOL HALL*

Deep in the country lush and green
where brown cows graze along
and tracks are gone or overgrown
and streams have lost their song
there stands Little Pool Hall
but no one comes to call.

A grey farmhouse with blinded eyes
and gaps where winds can sneak,
with gutters gone so rain can play
his games of drip and leak
over Little Pool Hall
and no one comes to call.

Damsons glow on the yellow trees
but no one picks the fruit.
Brambles and docks fill the borders-
the garden's destitute
behind Little Pool Hall,
and no one comes to call.

In an empty room with smooth floors
a solitary wooden chair
waits in the sparkle of dust-flecks
for someone to sit there
inside Little Pool Hall
but no one comes to call.

Weighed with cares did the farmer leave,
the last one of his kind,
as the old ways died and new ones came
to leave this place behind,
to leave Little Pool Hall
so no one comes to call?

When we called at Little Pool Hall
an old brown owl lived there.
She did not put a kettle on.
She did not seem to care
for Little Pool Hall
or that we came to call.

*Little Pool Hall is a derelict farmhouse
In Monmouthshire.

GRUMPY DOG

Grumpy dog
dozing in the dark.
Grumpy dog
does a little bark.
Jumpy, lumpy, humpy
bumpy, grumpy dog.

Grumpy dog
scratching at the door,
Grumpy dog
with an angry paw.
Lumpy, humpy, bumpy,
grumpy, jumpy dog.

Grumpy dog
isn't very pleased.
Grumpy dog
snapping at the leaves.
Humpy, bumpy, grumpy,
jumpy, lumpy, dog.

Grumpy dog
howling all day long.
Grumpy dog
not a catchy song.
Grumpy, jumpy, lumpy,
humpy, bumpy dog.

Grumpy dog
running round and round
Grumpy dog
with a growling sound.
Bumpy, grumpy, jumpy,
lumpy, humpy dog.

MORE BIRDS

Mild-eyed
and mottled
Dunnock
comes to call.

Red-eyed
and throttled
is Pheasant's
harsh call.

THE WEAK BOY

I threatened to hit the boy who
every one said was weak.
I stood right over him as he
went pale and could not speak.

I made that boy give me his crisps
and ate them while he gazed
then pushed him over to the ground
where he lay still and dazed.

A teacher came and asked him why
he lay there on the ground.
The weak boy said he'd fallen down
when running round and round.

By now that boy was scratched and bruised
but never snitched or cried.
He just took it all in silence
and, when questioned, he lied.

Walking home after school that day
I saw that boy once more.
His mum was shouting and pushing
him through his own back door.

When I got home juice and biscuits
were ready for my tea.
As I ate I started to think
he was stronger than me.

WOOD

Where the deer walks
where the bird hawks
where the wind talks
where the path forks
there the wood lurks.

Where the fox barks
where the eye sparks
where the bush darks
where the cold starks
there the wood murks.

WHEREVER

Wherever you go
in this swelling scene
if May is white
then June is green.

BONFIRE NIGHT

November the fifth.
                      Fireworks bloom.
Chance eruptions change the heavens,
sudden applauses sever the darkness
and flails of heat flog the cold night.

In the grasp of death is Guy the traitor;
bound to the bonfire he merrily burns,
an old enemy, enlarging in smoke.
Serpents of spark spit through the clouds
to a magical moon unmoved by the action.
Fire-dragon's claws drag at the sky
for her silver hoard that hangs far above.
Failing, the flames fizzle in despair
and scourge with spite the spent effigy.
Red teeth, tearing, turn into fragments
of blackness its boldness. The blazing fades.

Salvoes of squibs salute the execution
as the rockets sky-race and write their signs
of jaunty colours over this joyful scene.

A rosy orchard of ripened faces
peer the people, plumped up by autumn.

EVOLUTION 1

Mouse is bat
and bat is mouse
but bat flies off
just like that
and mouse scuttles
under a house.

EVOLUTION 2

A mouse is not
like a horse,
a horse is not
like a bat but
in mums' tums
they all have
whopping heads,
they all have
curly tails,
they all have
flipper arms,
they all go
swirly whirly.

STRIMMER WOMAN
MAKES FIRE

She cut the grass with
her red faced strimmer
and what she did next
turned grim to grimmer.
She lit up the heaps
of grass to glimmer
and cooked up a stink
to fizz and simmer.

I watched her carry
her loathsome luggage,
her armfuls of sickly
yellow baggage.
In the dead of night
she stirred this garbage
letting off a pong worse
than boiling cabbage.

Invisible flames
sent smoke seep-seeping
through open windows
and upstairs creeping.
The people wondered
what was reeking:
rotten fish, dog pooh
or lavatories leaking?

"I can't eat my dinner!"
"The washing's ruined!"
"You never know next
what she'll be brewing."
"She's coming back to
do more stewing."
"If this carries on
we'll all start spewing!"

THE DANDELIONS

Lining the highways,
turning the fields into gold –
the dandelions.

Full moons in the grass,
white parachutes everywhere –
the dandelions.

CAFETERIA

Most of us sit and sip.
Some of us lick and dip.

One fair woman with
a fine flourish produces
a chocolate gateau, singing
'Happy Birthday' to
a young man with a bottle
of champagne in his hand.
A party of friends gathers.

Most of us sit and sip.
Some of us lick and dip.

Watch out for the tall,
dark-haired lady, wearing
the blue uniform and
holding the magic spray
like a handgun while
staring at your empty cup.
She cannot wait to open fire
on your table *sput-sput-sput*
and wipe it jiffy clean!

Most of us sit and sip.
Some of us lick and dip.

On the silver counter are
glassed compartments
like television screens.
Would you like to watch
the Cheese and Chutney
Sandwich Show or the Dance
of the Cream Cakes, or maybe
a thriller starring lemon
and vanilla yoghurts?

Most of us sit and sip.
Some of us lick and dip.

A hungry young man
thumbs a phone call on
his wafer thin mobile,
opens wide his mouth
to speak then pops in
a scrummy jam tart.

Most of us sit and sip.
Some of us lick and dip.

WETTEST OF WETS

World is grunge -
all those sing along birdies
squelch like sponge.

Sky is sludge -
our back garden's turned into
chocolate fudge.

Fields are pools -
people with no umbrellas are
silly fools.

Roofs are drums -
kids get dragged into school by
drippy mums.

Trees pour drinks -
every drip that drops is an
eye that winks.

Grids are clogged -
clinging shirts and underpants
get well sogged.

LETTERBOX JEANS
(for Ollie Bennett)

My dad, Thom, is
a little bit scruffy.
His clothes are often
creasy and fluffy.

In his old jeans there's
a rip and a tear
that show hairy bits
of his legs all bare.

One day they looked
just like a letterbox
so I posted stuff like
straws and bits of rocks.

Grandad laughed and
Gran said, "Stitch 'em up!"
Dad walked on and never
even hitched 'em up.

SUPERMARKET BLUES

Young shelf stackers
wheeling their high rise piles
of cardboard boxes
blocking up the aisles
and queues, queues, queues
give me the Supermarket Blues.

Wild silver trolleys
snapping at my heels
with monstrous loads on
wibble-wobble wheels
and queues, queues, queues
give me the Supermarket Blues.

Family gatherings
sprawling over shelves,
thinking of no one else
but their selfish selves
and queues, queues, queues
give me the Supermarket Blues.

Shopping lists in writing
nobody could read
when I can never find
a single thing I need
and queues, queues, queues
give me the Supermarket Blues.

Arms that reach and snatch
right in front of my face
then I wander off
to find a quiet place
without queues, queues, queues
that give me the Supermarket Blues.

SLEEP
Day thoughts
ride into fog.
You don't see
them anymore
until they are
phantoms on
magic horses
doing deeds that
can't be done
as you stumble on
through the fog.

THE BUBBLE

We live in a bubble
to keep out of trouble.
Burst the bubble – do not hide.
Burst the bubble – step outside
and you will find
a jumble of notes in the afternoon
speckling the city with a sweet old tune;
the faint breeze of people hurrying down
the busiest street of the bustling town;
a tray of chips munched by a hungry one,
in threes and fours till gone is everyone.

We live in a bubble,
to keep out of trouble.
Burst the bubble – do not hide.
Burst the bubble – step outside
and you will find
flocks of girls wearing shoes like clown's stilts,
with chatters, totters, weird shapes, strange tilts;
muscle-bound tanned men covered in tattoos
who never make way, for they are the Yahoos;
one old lady who dropped all her shopping,
helped by a small boy, the only one stopping.

We live in a bubble,
to keep out of trouble.
Burst the bubble – do not hide.
Burst the bubble – step outside
and you will find
pearly drops of rain making crowds scurry
and pop up their brollies and hats in a hurry;
cafes and shops with wet people filling,
dripping their drops and round counters milling;
sunshine polishing up the round cobbles,
bringing folk back in dribbles and drobbles.

THE HILL

Ride the hill,
oh ride the hill
to where the dragon flies.

Ride until,
oh ride until
you hear his gurgling cries.

TEENAGE BROTHER'S
FIRST LOVE POEM

My brother came home
one day all dreamy,
instead of hard like
stone he was creamy.

He rushed to his room
with pen and notebook
wearing a weird and
far away ghost look.

I sneaked to his door
and heard him chanting,
which made a change from
his raving and ranting.

Later I saw this
poem on his screen,
in fancy font and
entitled 'Pauline'.

I read and giggled
at all this claptrap
written 'with love'
on my brother's laptop:

'Oh Pauline I love
your big brown eyes
that shine like two
bright conkers.

'Oh Pauline I love
your long black plaits
that hang down your
back like bellropes.

'Oh Pauline I love
your smooth white skin
that covers your pretty
face like chalk.'

That night he came home
looking like thunder.
Did he read that poem
to her, I wonder?

SOMEONE ELSE

"Mummy, what's it like
to be someone else?"
"Go and ask her, dear,
ask that Someone Else."

"Just like you but
different, happy and sad,
needing a friend like you,"
Someone Else said.

"Scared of not being
liked, sometimes angry, too,
wanting to share a joke
and fun, like you.

"Pleased with many of
the things I have got,
sorry if you have none
when I have a lot.

"Lonely in the night
when the curtain is drawn
and dreams turn to
nightmares before the dawn.

"That's what it's like
to be someone else," said
my new friend Someone
Else and I'm not sad.

TAKE-OFF

An aeroplane,
nose pointing
to the clouds,
flies out of
the roof of
a block of
flats where
flags also fly.

FROM ABOVE

From above
the white clouds
the world below
that once was
fields and cities
now is snow.

HOME TIME

Through the shrubs
toddlers creep.
In their prams
babies sleep.

Cars block
the school gate.
Patiently
mums wait.

Chairs scrape
over floors.
Kids fly
through the doors,

hands twirling
bags around,
mouths shrieking
freaky sounds.

It's just like
a pantomime
outside school
at home time.

ESTUARY

low tide
mast masses

> *strutting seagull*
> *puffs his chest out*
> *spotted wader*
> *pokes at nothing*
> *plummeting tern*
> *shatters water*

dull flats
bobbing buoys

> *seaweed wigs*
> *the baldy mud*
> *sucking clicks*
> *from wormy holes*
> *thirsty channels*
> *drain the marshes*

grey sea
boys crabbing

> *tall fairgirl*
> *cuts the samphire*
> *grounded lobsters*
> *lie in boxes*
> *slithery fishes*
> *squirm on counters*

steel sky
quiet voices
ropes for mooring
>   *slap together*
>   *bubbling curlews*
>   *fly in crescents*
>   *aeroplane drones*
>   *under the clouds*

TIME ZONES

Somewhere over the ocean
Somewhere up in the sky
Somebody stole my hours
And put them by.

Sometime when returning
Somewhere deep in the black
Someone else found my hours
And gave them back.

CASTLE

Grassy mound,
ditch all round,
quiet sound,
Castle.

Broken rocks,
solid blocks,
jackdaw flocks,
Castle.

Weedy walks,
seedy stalks,
hunting hawks,
Castle.

Tower steep,
gloomy deep,
long asleep
Castle.

Granite wall,
splendid hall,
battle call
Castle.

Kings and lords,
swarming hordes,
clash of swords
Castle.

Arrows fly,
wounded cry,
soldiers die
Castle.

Smoke and fire,
higher and higher,
falling spire
Castle.

BUZZARD

Light is the float
of the dark one,
lifting from
treetops barely
with effort,
leisurely surfing
the green fields
and crying, crying
mournfully.

TWO KIDS FOUGHT

Two kids fought:
they shouted and screamed
the most appalling things
and the two kids fought.

Two kids fought:
they kicked each other
till they were black and blue
and the two kids fought.

Two kids fought:
they punched each other
until the red blood ran
and the two kids fought.

Two kids fought:
they dragged each other's
clothes till they were ruined
and the two kids fought.

Two kids fought:
they battered themselves
to a weary standstill
and the two kids stopped.

Two kids stood:
they breathed heavily
and neither remembered
why the two kids fought.

SHE'S DIFFERENT

She's different, that girl-
she's not like us at all.
She's gawky, that girl-
she's bony, thin and tall.

She came to our school
from somewhere far away
with funny-coloured clothes.
I hoped she wouldn't stay.

She never looks at you but
stares at a far off place
with a twisted smile on her
blue-eyed, scrawny face.

She doesn't talk like us
but with a foreign sound
and none of the kids in
our class wants her around.

Sue made fun of her accent,
Jacky pulled at her hair.
I stood by and waited
to see if she would care.

That girl started crying -
a sob so long and deep.
Her bony shoulders shook -
it made me want to weep.

She crouched down in a corner
near the netball post.
Her bottom lip quivered -
she turned white as a ghost.

Something deep inside me
told me to go to her.
I touched her gently on
the arm and stroked her hair.

LIPSTICK LADY

Lipstick Lady, you
never like to munch.
You bypass your lips
when eating your lunch.
Lipstick Lady! Pass the gravy!

You slide the food off your
fork with careful teeth,
dropping it down to
your tongue underneath.
Lipstick Lady! Pass the gravy!

You chew as if speaking
a few chosen words
and the sounds you make
are as squeaky as birds.
Lipstick Lady! Pass the gravy!

You drink your wine
from an elegant glass
but can't help leaving
a great smudgy kiss.
Lipstick Lady! Pass the gravy!

THE WAVE

The wave rakes
the tinkling, winking stones.

The wave grinds
the briny, shiny bones.

The wave makes
the ridging, bridging beach.

The wave puts
tunes in the seagulls' beaks.

The wave shakes
the rattling, clattering shells.

The wave brings
the sound of distant bells.

The wave breaks
on rumbling, tumbling rocks.

The wave sends
a hundred, thousand shocks.

RAIN

When the rain comes
slanting down
it puts on every
face a frown.

It brings to streets
a creeping gloom
then makes the bright
umbrellas bloom.

On spinning tyres
it puts the swish,
in holiday heads
a sunshine wish.

As sky fills up
with misery clouds
the shops grow big
with grumpy crowds.

THE TEST

I was walking up the road
to Somewhere, whistling
a tune, not a care in the world
when I met a stern man
standing and staring.

He would not let me
pass unless I took his test.
I sat down as he opened
a black case and took out
sheaves of papers with
useless problems and
puzzles that I must answer.

It was like tangling
with wriggling snakes or
running fast into blanketty fog.
It was like being
terrorised in the dark
or being tied upside
down to the ceiling.

I fumbled over the test
and failed it, lost my whistle
and didn't know where to go,
sliding down the slippery
road to Nowhere.

COUNTING
FLOWERS

One snowdrop
breaks through winter:
spring's fresh sign.

Two daffodils'
golden trumpets
keep good time.

Three daisies
clear and silver
stand in a line.

Four buttercups:
look inside, you'll
see them shine.

Five dandelions:
blow the seeds
to tell the time.

Six speedwells
with little spots
in their eyes.

Seven bluebells
in the woods
so clear and fine.

Eight honeysuckles
smell as sweet
as summer wine.

Nine sweet peas
like open lips
up fences climb.

Ten red roses
on the briar
end my rhyme.

FLINTY PEBBLES

Flinty pebbles on the shore
Rattle where you walk.

Flinty pebbles when the sea
Washes them will talk.

DREAM POEM

The roaring rainbow,
the piercing lances
and three mad-flapping crows.

The narrowing tunnel,
the falling fences
and three red-hatted cows.

INDEX